C000212204

BEYOND THE MIND

JEMA FOWLER

Arkbound
Building futures, Bridging divides

Beyond the Mind
by Jema Fowler

© Jema Fowler

ISBN: 9781912092833

First published in 2020
by Arkbound Foundation (Publishers)

Arkbound is a social enterprise that aims to promote social inclusion, community development and artistic talent. It sponsors publications by disadvantaged authors and covers issues that engage wider social concerns. Arkbound fully embraces sustainability and environmental protection. It endeavours to use material that is renewable, recyclable or sourced from sustainable forest.

Arkbound
Rogart Street Campus
4 Rogart Street
Glasgow, G40 2AA

www.arkbound.com

BEYOND THE MIND

ACKNOWLEDGEMENTS

I would like to thank Amanda Thomas for helping me realise my dream of writing my book. I would also like to thank Arkbound and their staff for making it possible for me to publish my work and for helping me in every way they can. I'd also like to thank my amazing family and friends for always supporting me in everything I do and for believing in me. You are all so special to me. Also, thanks to James Urquhart who has helped me, supported me, pushed me to pursue my studies and made me believe in myself. I also want to mention a lady who I think has been a really influential writer - Rhonda Byrne. If you haven't already read her book *The Secret* order it now.

I have to thank other people for their part in my journey to enlightenment. My research and the information have come from many sources including from my online courses, internet research, and personal experiences. I must also thank my online tutors from my Mindfulness & Life Coaching courses by Joel & Natalie Rivera, my Law of Attraction course that is run by Graham Nicholls, and *The Study of Metaphysics* by Alfredo Rivera. The information I have learned from these courses through UDEMY have been invaluable to me and have given me the inspiration to write this book so that other people can learn this important information in a basic, simple and interesting way to show them how that can improve their mind-set and ultimately make their life so much better.

SURROUND
YOURSELF WITH
PEOPLE WHO
BELIEVE IN
YOU AND BRING
OUT THE BEST
IN YOU.

My name is Jema; I am a certified Mindfulness, Meditation & Life Coach. Continuously educating myself within my new life-coaching journey, I have studied subjects such as psychotherapy, emotional intelligence and metaphysics. I am going to help you heal, get motivated, feel more spiritual, be in optimum health and live your life to its full potential. I am going to change your mindset and your future. Don't be on your last legs wishing you could have another shot at life. Be on your last legs knowing you smashed life in peace, prosperity and maximum happiness. In this book you will learn how to pursue and experience the **best** you can in life. Don't wait until it's too late. You will **not** be scared of failure; don't live in fear or in the past, live in happiness and fulfilment by learning to understand emotion, use mindfulness and meditation to manifest your dreams. Be your highest version of you.

> YOU WILL ALWAYS BE ABLE TO MAKE MORE MONEY, BUT YOU CANNOT MAKE MORE TIME.
> – MORGAN FREEMAN

At the time of writing this book, the world has been plunged into turmoil as a global pandemic ravages the planet. It has been a time when many people have looked inwards, looking for resources that they are not sure they have, but which they need to come through this unprecedented time in our history. Now, more than ever, people are taking stock of their emotional and spiritual health, as long periods of isolation force them to become reacquainted with themselves. Suddenly what was 'OK' when they were too busy to take any notice of how things were going just won't do anymore. We all have a potential that few of us actually reach, so it is about learning how to reach a better self-awareness to create a more mindful future that we all deserve.

I first started to believe that there had to be more to life after a complex relationship break up. I found myself emotionally drained, which had me heading down the wrong path in life. I made bad decisions and lost everything I had worked for. I doubted my own emotions and beliefs. I have an amazingly supportive family and loving friends that helped me but there was still something keeping me from overcoming some of the emotional trauma I had experienced. I just didn't know how to move forward.

Doctors prescribed a whole raft of medication to help me sleep and to prevent panic attacks but that was not what I wanted. I decided to look at my issues from a more open-minded perspective and began to consider meditation as opposed to medication. I did not want medicine to mask my problems; I wanted to get to the bottom of what was wrong and fix it! I turned myself inside out, began working on my inner self, discovering I had more power and control than I had ever been made aware of.

I began to wake up to the idea that I could move on and begin to close doors. Learning how the mind works and accessing my inner spirit and mind on a deeper level allowed me to heal and work towards making the rest of my life fulfilling and happy. I started to study mindfulness and the law of attraction and I'm now experiencing prosperity - a love and connection beyond what I'd ever experienced before.

Despite the fact that most of our brain is active most of the time, as humans we only use a small percentage as we grow up. We are only programmed and taught to use what we need to ensure that we 'fit' into our place in society. We tend to live in either other peoples' experiences or our own past experiences rather than what we see, feel or want right now in this moment. People do have a tendency to "dumb down to society" copying and mimicking people and worrying about how other people see them - unconscious activity based on what we learn and see around us throughout our lives.

According to Sigmund Freud, our unconscious mind is what influences our behaviour and emotions. Neuroscientists have conducted studies that show that 95% of our cognitive activity is beyond our conscious awareness and only 5% is influenced by the conscious part of our brain.

We are certainly not taught about being mindful, and, apart from in the anatomical sense, we are taught nothing about how our brains work, how our emotions are processed or how to manage them. We are not taught how to deal with stress or shown how we can overcome trauma. We are thought to be the most intelligent beings on the planet, and we have the capability to use so much more of our brains than we do, thereby becoming more in tune with the universe we live in. Indeed, some people have done that by exploring beyond the everyday to discover different ways of thinking and being. By connecting our brains and our body we can achieve so much more.

By practicing mindfulness and achieving harmony with your mind, body and spirit, you can obtain love, happiness & abundance that you could only ever have dreamed of. You can always tell a person who is practicing mindfulness, as they will be serene and unflappable, and always seem to be in control of their emotions. During the current Coronavirus crisis, we do not have to look very far to find people who are practicing mindfulness, whether they know it or not. The doctor who risks his life to treat sick people, isolating himself from his own family and their support; the nurse who holds the hand of a dying patient who, because of the virus, is not able to be with her family, and makes the last moment for that patient and their relatives the best that she can. Consider that doctor's calmness and ability to manage her own emotions, safe in the knowledge that someone's need is greater than her own. This is mindfulness. However, being actively mindful for your own wellbeing takes practice. You must practice on a daily basis purposefully, creating positive habits and accepting "what is" and not burying or suppressing emotion. It's not just about subconsciously being able to switch off at work. What about when you're at home, exhausted and emotionally drained from helping others? By practicing being mindful you will learn not only to manage emotion but to live in the present and not allow bad experiences to take a hold in your unconscious mind, draining you and effecting your life. How many of you have struggled during isolation, surrounded by panic and negativity, scared and unmotivated, unable to see family, meet new people, progress at the gym or at work? Guess what? You needed that break, you needed that scare to make you realise we do not get a second chance at life.

Now is the time to be the best you can, accept and let go of that emotion and worry. You have no control over a pandemic, but you have control over your own mind and your outcomes from this. You are rested, and ready for round two of your precious life. You cannot buy back time, but you can make the rest of your life count! If you want to change your job CHANGE IT; if you want to fix a relationship FIX IT; if you feel stuck and stagnant DO SOMETHING ABOUT IT. In this pandemic, realise that we all need to reflect and rest; the planet has definitely benefited from a rest from our attempts to destroy it, so let's work on living instead of dying, bringing life instead of despair, being positive instead of toxic and letting go of all of that poison that you have collected over the years. Let go of negativity, let go of bitterness, jealousy & fear.

Now let me show you the result of many hours of studying and practice. Let me help you to awaken yourself and begin to live your best life.

CHAPTER ONE

*Your soul is screaming for you
to answer your true calling.*
— Morgan Freeman

There is no short cut to achieving success and I was determined that what I offered to my clients would be informed by many hours of study covering multiple subjects that relate to the human mind. The result is this book. It incorporates information from my studies in Life Coaching, Mindfulness, Meditation, Emotional Intelligence & the Law of Attraction. It also comes from a deep understanding of these subjects and a drive to help my clients to achieve the best result that they can.

Take back control

As we work through these topics together you will start to notice a change in your habits. You will then be able to control your emotions and you will be able to incorporate mindfulness and meditation into your daily schedule. From there it will be a short step to your dream life. The aim will always be for my clients to experience fulfilment, happiness, love and abundance to its full potential throughout their lives ensuring that negative emotions and the unconscious mind do not prevent progress.

Mindfulness can be a powerful thing. This is Jess's story. Jess remembers the day she was just about to turn 23 and was in her first job, and crossing the courtyard going back to her desk after her lunch break. Suddenly a deep feeling of fearfulness gripped her, paralysing her. Jess was shaken but hoped it had been a one off. It wasn't. Each time Jess was sent home, her father left her in no doubt that he thought Jess was making it up. Nobody in the family even wanted to mention it. Jess felt very alone.

Things got worse for Jess after she got a promotion. Her anxiety was getting in the way of her work and she felt she had let her team down. Her parents finally realised that something was wrong, and Jess left her job and returned home.

At home all the time, agoraphobia set in. Jess spent her days in the house reading, playing video games or watching hours of TV. Her anxiety got worse and she suffered from severe feelings of fear as well as some debilitating physical symptoms.

Cognitive behavioural therapy (CBT)

Jess went to a support group, a one-to-one version of the support group, and also had CBT. In the support group the focus was on dealing with stress and drummed into Jess the benefits of exercise and healthy living to combat mental health problems. It left her unmoved. The one-to-one support group didn't help either, with nothing new to offer her although Jess found the CBT did help with her agoraphobia.

Mindfulness

It was when Jess was seen by the local mental health and wellbeing group that the mention of mindfulness first came up. She was less than enthusiastic and thought it might be all a bit airy-fairy. Breathing deeply and thinking happy thoughts wouldn't help her, would it?

Jess dragged herself to the first session and after that, everything changed. Now mindfulness is built into Jess's life every day. She finds the breathing and the meditation and imagery help her most and she uses them at least twice a day.

Looking at things with fresh eyes

Since she started practicing mindfulness, Jess is more positive with a new perspective of what is really important in her life. She feels stronger and is more resilient and able to handle life's daily pressures. Where she once used to block everything out of her mind, she now deals with everything as it comes along with it head on. Jess is convinced that mindfulness and all that goes with it is a really powerful, but an undervalued tool.

How can cultivating mindfulness and self-awareness improve my life?

- Mindfulness can extend, improve and allow you to enjoy more of your life.
- You learn to manage your thoughts and emotions.
- You develop peace of mind.
- Enable you to live a happier, healthier, awakened life.
- Reduces stress and anxiety.
- Gives you self-compassion and control.
- You have improved energy levels.
- You will sleep better.
- You will dream bigger.

- You will improve your immune system.
- You will have the ability to be focused.

Mindfulness and mindset

Let's just look at what mindfulness is. It is one of the key aspects to happiness and fulfilment, so we need to have a long hard look at it.

To be mindful is to purposefully bring your attention to the present moment without judgement. Mindfulness is practiced through meditation and other techniques that we will be discussed here

As human beings, we have a bad habit of focusing our attention on the past, regretting choices that we have made or worrying about the future and what it has in store for us. And when we are not worrying about that, we are worrying about other people's opinions. This is because generally our minds are on autopilot and our unconscious mind just takes over our daily lives relying on the old tried and tested responses and doing what we have always done. We are pushed and pulled, by the experiences and emotions we have. The problem is that no one ever taught us why we feel those emotions and how we control them before they start to affect our health.

Past Experiences

Emotions are the product of our past experiences. That is because we live by a memorised set of behaviours and thoughts that we have learned throughout our lives. This is the place our fear and worry come from and that in turn is what holds us back and makes us want to retreat to our "safe place". If we can become more mindful and live more in the present, we can change these habitual thoughts, but it takes time and consistency. Following mindfulness practices, however, definitely has the potential to change your life.

We live in a society where it is hard not to become obsessed with controlling every outcome and every situation and in doing so we think we are creating or living the life we want - but are we really? Are we creating what we believe is our perfect life or are we trying to create something that we think other people consider to be the perfect life? Is it really possible to control everything? The answer is no. When we try to control every outcome, we take ourselves away from the power of the universe and let fear take over. Fear of imperfection, fear of what other people might think, fear of things not going the way we want them to, and even fear of the past. People will start to see chaos and stress in their lives and soon begin to feel there is nothing more to life if they cannot find a way to change this learned behaviour.

We need to stop comparing ourselves to other people. Find the courage to block out the clamour of society, silence the noise and negativity around us and the constant "what ifs." We can make our time here count, or we can live in fear and worry about the bad things that happen in the world that we have no control of. We can mentor and lead people to happiness and make a difference in the world in our own way, but first we need to turn ourselves inside out. It takes discipline, courage and persistence to do this, but these are skills we are naturally born with.

You can do this!

The truth is that you can't buy another life or buy extra time. You just can't put a price on life or happiness. You will make the time if you want to be the best and happiest you can be and if you want to live your life and not just go through the motions. Inspire people, teach people, set an example. You will believe that you can do anything. You must become completely focused on self-improvement and challenging yourself to be the best you can be, why stop learning? Why have limits?

But remember, if you want to succeed you must learn to fail. Every transition in life gets harder before it gets better. If you're reading this... you have just done your "harder" and now that's in the past. The hardest bit no longer exists because now you are motivated to better yourself and live in the present moment, not the past. You will succeed and your mindset will become unstoppable.

CHAPTER TWO

*You can learn and change in a state of
pain and suffering or you can learn and
change in a state of joy and inspiration.*
— Dr Joe Dispenza

The effects of COVID-19 & emotional trauma

As the Coronavirus pandemic ravages the world that we live in, it is only to be expected that just as people have been feeling during the height of the crisis, after lockdown there will be some people who will continue to feel anxiety, stress and fear. Some may even experience agoraphobia as the rules are relaxed and more people are out and about and returning to work. For others, the enforced lockdown may have given them time to reflect on their lives. Many will feel the need for a change. Some will already have acted on this and started to make adjustments to the way they live and the way they think about themselves.,. For others, although they recognise that some positive changes are needed in their lives, they may be too scared to and act and end up procrastinating due to their fear of change.

Don't fear change – it's healthy!

As we consider what changes we can make in our lives after the lessons we've learned over the months that have been overshadowed by the effects of a global pandemic, it is worth knowing that change is one of the healthiest things that we can do, especially when we feel stagnant, unfulfilled or unhappy. However, it is also true that we tend to avoid it. Even if we acknowledge that things need to change, it can take years for us to act upon that instinct.

Change is GOOD.

Change will get you off that hamster wheel.

The other thing we need to bear in mind is that we all need to take risks to succeed. In fact, we must be prepared to fail first to enable us to go on and succeed and we must always be driven and have a vision of how we want our lives to be that we can refer to as a guide.

Don't forget that fear, anxiety and stress are generally feelings you get that are based on an opinion and a judgement of a situation rather than the actual fact, and this is where we all have a tendency to go wrong. We are letting our bodies go into fight or flight mode, exhausting ourselves and allowing a bad mindset to develop based on something that isn't even really happening.

The human instinct is driven by automatic responses in our brain that are developed when we do something multiple times, forming neural pathways that allow our bodies to carry out the action automatically.

The responses of worry and fear are normal and, indeed, essential responses to keep us safe and to help us avoid potentially harmful situations. They happen automatically following a perceived threat because we don't spend enough time purposefully thinking about that threat in our conscious minds.

Emphasise the positive

Because our thought system is complex and influential to us don't let your first thought in the morning be a negative one linked to an unfortunate or upsetting memory. Don't allow your thoughts to tether you constantly to the past. Now that the effects of Coronavirus appear to be less imminent, we need to shift our thoughts to the present and our vision to our future, rather than dwelling on very sad and worrying times that we've just been through. Put simply, if you had a stressful day yesterday, don't let that impact on you today. Make a conscious effort to make your state of being and mind-set in the moment relevant to today. If you don't, and you dwell on the negativity, disappointments or stress that you encountered yesterday will trickle into days to come. Remember the law of attraction? Whatever you have in your hearts and in your mind is what you will attract to yourself.

If you suffered the tragedy of losing a loved one during this pandemic, then as hard as it might be, you must try to release your emotion and then live your best life for them, because in your heart you know that they would not wish for you to be living in fear and sadness for the rest of your life. If you can't do it yourself, then think of their sacrifice, and do it for them.

If you feel anxious about going back to work because you don't want to be there and your time at home has brought that into focus, then look more deeply into the reason for this. If you analyse your feelings and find out what is really behind your reluctance is that you don't like your job, this is your perfect opportunity to change it.

On the other hand, if you look into your heart and the reason for your reluctance is because you feel anxious or agoraphobic because you're worried about something, think about what that might be. Is it because you don't want to see certain people there? Maybe the fact is that you fear that work might be slow, or you may lose clients, or you might not have enough work? If this is what is making you anxious, then it is time to change your mindset. Trust me - if you can change your mind-set from negative to positive it will change your life.

If you have feelings of agoraphobia and anxiety, they may stem from what you see and hear on social media, the news and what people say **could happen** or rumours of the things that have happened to other people. Often these are not facts and do not reflect the **current** situation in **your** life. You cannot expect to lead a happy and fulfilled healthy life if you are constantly haunted by thoughts that you might get hurt or fall ill. Even on your darkest days try to think about the fact that you are fine and try to appreciate the things and people you still have in your life. Hold on to whatever brings you comfort. When things are difficult you will be able to deal with them. Then after you have dealt with them you can learn to accept that they happened, and you can let them go.

You will do this because not only will stress and worry have a very bad effect on your health and attract more negativity. Do not leave it too late to realise that you have spent your whole life worrying often more than is necessary or just because you were falling into step with what everyone else was concerned about.

Long term memories and our emotions

Long term memories are formed when we are in a highly emotional state. If it's a negative emotion, then this will trap you within the boundaries of those emotions. This means that if you have experienced high levels of stress and emotional trauma, this is what has given rise to your embedded memories and you will now have to work on your emotional reaction. This may sound as though it will be easier said than done but it is vitally important that you do not allow the emotional reaction to that memory of a previous trauma to last for too long by living in the past and continually revisiting events in your mind. If you allow this destructive pattern of being overwhelmed by negative emotion to continue, then it will progress and become part of your temperament that will begin to define you. In the worst-case scenario if you allow yourself to dwell on the negative thoughts for years it will then become an embedded personality trait. We have all met people who bring us down because of their negativity. They never seem to have a good word to say about anything or anyone and always appear very bitter or overcritical. These people, if we were to examine their past, would most likely have suffered a traumatic event, which they have allowed to overwhelm them and eventually define their personality. This is very damaging because it drives people away from us. That friend who is always 'glass half empty' and always looks on the worst side of everything is not somebody you're going to want to spend a lot of time around.

That is why it's so important to learn how to heal ourselves from trauma so that we are not stuck in a kind of Groundhog Day existence where we are reliving the trauma over and over again until it becomes our constant persona. Getting stuck in this negative mind-set and reliving the pain over and over again is damaging to you and to your body and there is no doubt that it will ultimately hinder your life.

This is where you need to take command of your unconscious mind. It will automatically try to encourage you to do this, because this is an automatic survival response in the brain set to react to trauma However, you can change this and instead allow your body to come out of the constant exhausting survival mode by being mindful and using meditation to alter the way that your brain deals with the repeated emotional trauma that it keeps reliving. The secret to this is to not allow your mind to keep anticipating the worst case scenario and when negative thoughts or memories threaten to intrude, ensure that you do not emotionally embrace that thought or feed it by giving it excessive attention. Turn your mind to other things and you'll soon find a new neural pathway has been formed that will automatically take you away from dwelling on negativity.

There have been many expected and unexpected bonuses and also less favourable things that lockdown has brought us. For a start it has rested our planet, revived nature, cleaned our sea and rivers, cleaned the air and given us a much-needed rest from the hustle and bustle of our frantic societies. We may have got to spend more time with loved ones and have more time for reflection. Perhaps we were able to use those things as a detox for our minds, bodies and souls? Equally, we may have experienced stress, sadness, anger and other negative emotions as well. Maybe you have got into unhealthy habits throughout lockdown but now you see that it is the time to put your body into optimum health and not take life and your health for granted, ever again.

A mindful approach will help you with almost any situation in your life. Even the worst situation can be mitigated by taking a mindful approach and using meditation to help restore peace to your life. The secret is to have gratitude for the things in your life that you are blessed with and to be positive even when things are looking pretty bleak. There always is a bright side to look on! You will also need to have a clear vision of your goals and work on devising what that is for you. It is definitely worth persevering through meditation and mindfulness to arrive at that place where you have achieved clarity. Clarity breeds serenity.

In summary, if you have experienced emotional trauma, you will need to make a conscious effort not to live inside that trauma and let it define you for the rest of your life. Instead, be mindful, meditate and radiate love. Make it your focus to help others and live consciously. Keep your negative thoughts at bay and encourage the more positive ones that are going to lead you to the fulfilment of your vision for yourself.

CHAPTER THREE

TAKING BACK CONTROL

People usually consider walking on water or in thin air a miracle. But I think the real miracle is not to walk either on water or in thin air, but to walk on earth. Every day we are engaged in a miracle which we don't even recognize: a blue sky, white clouds, green leaves, the black, curious eyes of a child— our own two eyes. All is a miracle.

— Thich Nhat Hanh

Now that we know what mindfulness is, let's think about what it would be like if we could control our thought processes, understand our emotions, manifest our dreams and live in happiness, love and abundance without struggle. This can be achieved through mindfulness. In order to attract positivity, we must avoid negativity. We attract what we feel and being more mindful of this will achieve great results. If you are constantly worrying about debt, then you will attract more of it. If you are worrying about someone hurting you, you can be sure that they will. If you are constantly thinking about negative things, more negativity is what you will attract. Now I can show you how we can change this by adapting our thought process.

This is how mindfulness can change lives. This is John's story: *John found his mind filled with the re-running of a time in his life that had been very distressing. He struggled to get over this destructive way of thinking and needed to train his mind to come back to the present and leave the bad memories behind. John needed some space between himself and the memories that haunted him. Having anxious and repetitive thoughts can be exhausting. John started to explore mindfulness and found that when he practiced it, even when the thoughts did overwhelm him, they were less impactful and threatening. He came to realise that just because the thoughts crept into his mind did not mean he had to give them credence. John was beginning to take back control. He joined a group of people seeking to deal with trauma through mindfulness and found that like him, many were plagued by the intrusive thoughts brought on by deep wounding. Using mindfulness, suddenly the thoughts took less time to pass and carried less terror. John was encouraged to write his story and then relay it within the group. He found that the story he told affected him less with his mindfulness approach. John came to realise that what had happened to him would never go away but by using the practices he had learned; he would be able to compartmentalise the feelings that had threatened to overwhelm him and deal with them more appropriately.*

Turn your doubts into DETERMINATION

So how can cultivating mindfulness and self-awareness allow us, like John, to improve our lives?

- Mindfulness can extend, improve and allow you to enjoy more of your life and help us to get our thought processes under control.
- You can learn to manage your thoughts and emotions. Like John you will not be overwhelmed by thoughts that haunt you from your past.
- As you manage your emotions and feelings and become able to deal with them, you will be able to develop peace of mind.
- Success with your mindfulness will enable you to live a happier, healthier, more awakened life.
- As you control your emotions and feelings you will find the everyday stress and anxiety of your life reducing.

- Your new understanding and mindfulness will give you self-compassion and self-control (a lot of rash and callous decision making comes from unhappiness).
- As your mindfulness abilities increase, so will your sleep and energy levels. Your body will respond physically to the effects of mindfulness with an improved immune system.
- Greater mindfulness will allow you to be more in control of everything in your life and allow better focus in everything you do.

Where do our negative thoughts come from?

The negative thoughts we have, like the ones that plagued John are the product of a bad habit. Although we use our conscious mind when we are focusing on something, the rest of the time we will live most of our lives on autopilot listening and reacting to our subconscious. That makes us worry, feel guilty and think those disruptive thoughts about past experiences that are no longer in the present and should have less ability to affect us.

This is a behaviour pattern most of us have been programmed into by the society we live in. This pattern is reiterated in school and work, and with family and friends because they too are stuck in the same "human programming" process. It's not anyone's fault, it's simply the way our society works. For example, when we are growing up we are always told to be careful and to make sure that we have 'something to fall back on', have a plan, stick to the same career, choose our education wisely. We are told that we might not get a second chance at it, so we better toe the line the first time. Naturally this makes us uncomfortable with the idea of change or taking risks even when they might improve our lives. However, you can learn new subjects and change your career and your life at any point. What you need is the ability to break through those barriers and form a positive, "can do" mindset.

Being unaware of our unconscious thoughts means we can't stop our, "thought demons" turning into an emotion. When we begin to focus less on our thoughts and more on the present then we can prevent our brain going into 'fight or flight mode' continuously. When the brain does this, it releases too many chemicals that go on to make us feel scared, worried, anxious or generally unwell. This will be covered in more detail later in the chapter.

The thought demon – my unconscious mind sending me bad thoughts

Our brains don't know the difference between thought and reality. For example, have you ever had a bad dream and woke up sweating or shaking? This is because the experience in your dream is interpreted by your brain as something that is actually happening, and it is either in fight or flight mode. That could be anything from preparing your digestion system to eat or preparing to fight for your very survival. Your body reacts because your brain sends the same signals it would if the situation was happening in reality rather than in a dream or thought.

Try this. Close your eyes and focus on the fact that you have a lemon in your hands. Now imagine cutting a slice of lemon and biting into it, sucking out the juice. Is your mouth watering? This is because as you picture the lemon your brain sends signals out to prepare for it getting you ready to eat and digest that lemon. Your brain will also trigger signals to your digestive system to break down the acids in the lemon. Your brain is super sensitive, intricately complex and highly intelligent. Learning how the mind works can give you reassurance when you have negative thoughts by enabling you to remind yourself that everything is OK and what you are experiencing is "just a thought".

What can I do to be mindful?

- Acknowledge that your brain can work unconsciously. Take your time to think about it and identify anything that might be causing problems.

- Self-observation – observe how your thought is making you feel. Really get in touch with your emotions and understand and identify the effect a negative thought has on you.

- Self-awareness – where are you right now? Are you ok? Are you in danger? Evaluate your situation and reassure yourself that everything is under control, you are safe and well and you are under no threat.

- Do you want to think about the passing negative thought, or would you like to dismiss it from your mind?
- Change your thought by focusing on something else – the most effective way of doing this is to meditate (more on this in chapter 5). Prepare and then use a short meditation to steer your attention towards something else if you're struggling to actively change your thoughts. Choose better feeling emotions and make better decisions.

It takes 90 seconds for a thought to turn into an emotion and then 90 seconds to hold an emotion if we don't feed into it.

Feeding an emotion means giving it thought. If you have a feeling of anger, anxiety or sadness and you go on to feed these thoughts they will snowball into something bigger when in fact **you have the ability to stop an emotion in its tracks**.

Don't give that negative emotion the oxygen of your thought, deprive it and it will die. We all know people, or maybe even we ourselves are prone to obsessing over negative thoughts. Let's say that someone that you know has upset you and an argument ensues. You are angry and hurt about it. What happens? You go over and over it in your mind, what she said, what you said, what you should have said, and how dare she speak to you like that? Before you know it, you have worked yourself up into such a state that you have physical symptoms like a clenched feeling in your stomach and a headache. You have given that negative emotion oxygen as if it was a fire and that oxygen has fanned it into a blaze that is consuming you. I am not unrealistic enough to think that upsetting row will not ever enter your mind, it will, but it is what you do when it does that will make the difference. Acknowledge it and dismiss it. That is what we mean by mindfulness.

MINDFULNESS -
A STATE OF HEIGHTENED AWARENESS AND
DELIBERATE FOCUS ON THE PRESENT MOMENT.

MEDITATION -
A MORE SPECIFIC PROCESS DIRECTED INTERNALLY
RATHER THAN OBSERVING THE OUTSIDE WORLD
AND PRACTICED DELIBERATELY.

Both practices focus on calming the mind and creating peace of mind that will benefit the body and the soul. Practicing mindfulness and meditation will enable you to reduce your level of thinking. It will not force you to completely stop thinking, you will just be able to control your train of thought better.

DID YOU KNOW OUR BRAINS SPECIFICALLY
FOCUS ON NEGATIVITY SO WE CAN MINIMISE
PAIN AND GO INTO SURVIVAL MODE QUICKER?

Let me give you an example: you are walking through a dark forest and hear a noise. Our human instinct takes over: Is that noise a sign of something dangerous? Is that something that can hurt me?

Following this encounter, we instinctively go into fight or flight mode and our brains release a chemical called adrenaline. The 'fight or flight mode' is the hard-wired survival mechanism in our brain that sends signals and releases the chemicals such as adrenaline.

The fight-or-flight response is also known as the acute stress response, and this refers to the physiological reaction we experience when something terrifies us. Hormones are released that will allow the brain to decide whether you are going to stay and deal with the situation (fight) or run to safety (flight).

What happens during the fight-or-flight response?

The heart rate, blood pressure, and breathing rate will increase, preparing our body to run or to fight. Once the threat is over, it will take anywhere from 20 to 60 minutes for our bodies to return to the levels they were at before the shock or threat we faced.

Being in a constant state of fight or flight can be very exhausting as the brain naturally assumes and the worst and prepares for it to minimise risk and pain. This is a basic animal instinct developed by our cave dwelling ancestors who experienced life threatening situations daily. In contemporary society, the fight or flight response can be much more nuanced and is our instinctive reaction to stressful situations. Where it used to be an essential tool for survival, it is now often something that we must control in order to dispel negative thoughts. Being in fight or flight mode all the time is draining because our brains release chemicals through neurotransmitters (chemical messages through cells) ready to protect us that have both short and long term effects on the body and brain such as sweating, rapid heart rate, pain, tension, trembling and dilated pupils (to allow for better vision in fight or flight mode). You will experience emotions such as fear, anxiety and sadness and then secondary feelings such as shame or anger. These emotions affect your memory and blood pressure and can cause digestive problems, chronic stress and even an increased risk of disease.

If you have a tendency to start the process of thinking negatively and forcing yourself into a heightened state resulting in fight or flight, then becoming aware of that tendency is the first step. It is possible for you to choose your response to situations rather than be catapulted into them by your uncontrolled thought processes. This negative and irrational way of thinking is also referred to as "the psychology of the monkey mind" or "mindlessness."

We have learnt that emotional reactions are not always aligned with what is happening in reality and it is very possible that you may feel anxious or upset when there is no immediate threat.

We have also learned that our brain triggers every emotion we feel by releasing chemicals and producing hormones. Our automatic response to fear predisposes us to negative thoughts. Fear is a defence mechanism allowing the most negative interpretation of a situation to forewarn us. Another complication is that we tend to judge and interpret situations based on the beliefs and opinions of others. The bottom line is that we need to be able to recognise our emotions, Identify the thoughts that emotion attracts, change those thoughts which in turn will change the emotion. We can control this, and we **can** change this.

By learning to acknowledge that we cannot control our unconscious mind we can learn to use our conscious thinking to use positive thoughts to change how we interpret or feel about a situation.

CHAPTER FOUR

I don't want to be at the mercy of my emotions. I want to
use them, to enjoy them, and to dominate them.
— Oscar Wilde

Emotions - we all have them and they create different behaviours in us based on how we feel. We can change our response from irrational to measured. To fully be in control of your emotions you will need to change and redirect your thinking and interpret your thoughts differently. Here is an example; imagine the moment you have a passing thought of a previous bad experience and then you start to think:

"What if this happens to me again? What if it comes back? Will it really hurt me and still affect me?"

Suddenly the thought of that previous bad experience threatens to take over. You need to stop it and change this thought to something like:

"Yes, that previous experience was bad, but it can't hurt me again. It has gone. I accept it happened and I accept it was a difficult time in my life, but now I am moving forward. Right at this moment I am safe, I am happy, and I am excited for the future."

Once you have overshadowed the negative thought then you can begin to think consciously and deliberately about something more positive.

There will always be moments in life that we have to live through that are hard, scary and painful. We all have emotions and there is no doubt that over our lifetime we will go through periods of anxiety, embarrassment, anger, grief, stress and many other negative emotions. That is what being human means and it is something that we can either let completely engulf us or learn how to control and respond to appropriately.

Seeking Solace

When we are going through negative emotions, we will naturally want to escape the pain and somehow push it away or blot it out. We might begin to try and get away from it or distract and divert ourselves by doing something else. We might drink too much or eat in excess in our attempt to replace that unresolved pain with something else.

Avoiding the pain rather than dealing with it will prolong your suffering and ultimately stop you from leading the life that you deserve to live.

Turn pain into strength with mindfulness

When you practice mindfulness, you will learn the way that you can turn any negative emotion into a source of strength and something that you can learn from. Rather than trying to ignore the trauma and avoid it we need to gently look towards the reasons that we are in pain and from there learn how to make the best choices. These choices will help us arrive at a better outcome than the constant turmoil of pain. It is only when we acknowledge this negativity that we can begin to heal.

Here is my seven-step guide that sums up what we need to do when negative emotions threaten us.

1. Stop, and acknowledge

When the negative feeling comes into your consciousness, you need to stop for a minute and then take a long deep breath. Acknowledge the feeling, no more, no less, don't give it the power to go further but don't deny its existence either.

2. Give it a name

Now that you have acknowledged the emotion is there then give it a name. Are you embarrassed? Ashamed? Accept that the emotion is in you.

3. Accept it

If you are ashamed or regretful, then admit to yourself that you are experiencing that emotion and that you accept that for the time being. This will work far better than punishing yourself for how you are feeling. Open yourself to it and then recognising it for what it is, is crucial. Now you will create a space around it in your thinking, and you will find out that the emotion you are feeling does not define you.

4. It's not forever!

Remember that no emotion is there forever. They will come up and then die down again, just like waves rolling in and out on the beach. So, let that wave roll into your mind, linger a moment and then withdraw again. With mindfulness you will be able to see these roll-in emotional waves as temporary.

5. Investigate and Respond

Once you have become calm and identified your visiting emotion, you will be in a good place to take a harder look at the emotion and to understand how it came to be and what about it is discomforting you. Maybe someone made a passing comment that you have taken personally and feel very embarrassed about. Take another look at it. Did they really mean to aim it at you or was it just a general comment? Often when you unpack the emotion you will see that the feeling it has set up in you was not the right response. Then you can let it go.

6. Avoid bad and destructive thinking.

Here's an example of a destructive thought habit:
Jenny was very excited to be going on holiday and was constantly saying, "I can't wait to be on holiday, oh it is

going to be so wonderful, sitting on the beach in the sun, that's all I want. I just know that I am going to be so happy when I get there."

Two weeks later Jenny was sitting on the beach with her friends but instead of enjoying the long-awaited holiday, Jenny spent the whole time talking about the unexpected breakup she had just had with her boyfriend which had upset her. Now instead of loving the holiday she had been looking forward to she was in a low and very negative mindset. After bemoaning the end of her relationship endlessly, Jenny started to focus on the end of the holiday;

"I don't want to go home. I'm dreading going back to work and seeing him" she wailed to her long-suffering friends.

Now Jenny was in an even more uncomfortable, anxious mindset. She was not even aware that she was still on a beautiful beach with her friends having the holiday that she had been so excited about.

By thinking that way, Jenny gave away her power and she allowed her unconscious mind to wonder and overthink the events in her past and worry about the future instead of enjoying where she was and what she was doing in that moment. Do you want your life to go by in a constant state of negativity? You have the choice to change your thoughts and not feed them. If you live in the mindset "I won't be happy until" or "I'll be happy when" generally you will never get to experience that emotion to its full potential, even when the thing you long for finally happens.

The truth is that sometimes we attach ourselves to our problems and by doing that we prevent ourselves from moving forward and ultimately being happy.

7. Trust yourself!

The better you get at your mindfulness the more you will be able to trust your response to emotions and the more confident you will be in dealing with them.

Meditation

Meditation practice can help redirect your mind. Some of the most influential and successful people on the planet use meditation practice on a daily basis to refocus, quiet the mind and reset. People like: Bill Gates, Michael Jordan, Will Smith, Jennifer Lopez, Sheryl Crow, Ellen DeGeneres, and Katy Perry.

Rhonda Byrne[1] describes how meditation is one of the key secrets to a life of fulfilment, happiness and emotional control. Byrne explains that, "meditation quizzes your mind, helps you control your thoughts, and revitalises your body". Meditation is a powerful tool with which you can take back control over your thoughts and emotions. The good news is that you can do this in as little as 5 minutes a day.

---

1   *The Secret* - Rhona Byrne

It's your choice

You have a conscious choice to make a decision to move forward and regain control of your life or to be held back in the past or fear for the future, drowning in negative emotions that can swallow you up like quicksand.

Overthinking the past and worrying about the future can be really destructive to your life. Learn to deal with your thoughts before overthinking leads to a bad emotional response or reaction.

Conscious and unconscious thinking

We have already said that thinking is what creates our emotions...and we are **always** thinking. So, it is not a matter of shutting down our brain, that simply can't happen, but we can deliberately practice how we want to feel and react when those negative thoughts come along and we can also practice living in the present moment.

Recognise that you have a choice

We have the ability to feel the way we want to, without needing to set any conditions and give in to any random emotion that comes along to derail us. Mindfulness can give us everything we need to deal with emotion in a positive way.

Practice being happy

Did you know there are ways to practice being happy and naturally encourage your body to release your happy hormones? More on this later.

Dream? Reality? Your brain doesn't have a clue!

For a moment let's come back to the fact that your brain doesn't know the difference between a dream and a reality.

Now let's try an exercise.
Write down your life dream and include all the things you want to feel emotionally, the materialistic things that you may want, maybe a dream house that you can live in with your loved one. Next, imagine how you will feel when this dream becomes a reality.

- What emotion will you feel?
- What feeling will you get from it?

Ultimately you want this dream to come true because of how good it will make you feel. Try to envision the emotion and really focus on how that emotion feels for a few minutes. Then acknowledge the feelings you get from thinking about it and feel the sensations and emotions that go with that. This is also a practice used in 'The Law of Attraction' to manifest your dreams. What you envision you will attract.

Go in depth when you are using this practice. Write it down with all the detail you can, things like.

IF YOU SEE IT IN YOUR MIND, YOU ARE GOING TO HOLD IT IN YOUR HAND.

- BOB PROCTOR

- What you are wearing.
- The car that you have on the drive.
- The person you are with.
- The place you are in.

But just remember that this premise is true of bad thoughts as well as good! If you allow negative thoughts to become the way you think then you will attract negative outcomes because you have fed the negative thought.

Write it down

Writing things down and journaling is always going to be a key factor to observing your thought process and tracking your progress and ultimately planning your new dream life. Putting things on paper can make it clearer for you to understand and monitor your progress. For example;

- If you feel a negative emotion and start to feel sad, write it down. Then ask yourself, is this something that is relevant today? Or is it something that belongs in the past? Or is it merely just a worry or a "what if?"
- Next write down how this makes you feel and then accept it. Say in your head, "I accept this but I am moving on from this as its not relevant to today".
- Acknowledge this is just a thought demon in your unconscious mind.
- Change the thought (maybe even on paper).
- Write down how you feel after changing that thought.

Do you feel different about the thought and about its relevance today?

The half-smile technique

Did you know that by smiling, even if you're not feeling particularly happy inside your body will interpret this as a movement you only do when you're feeling upbeat and it will release the same chemical as if you were actually cheerful? This increases your happy hormones, (endorphins) and contributes to a more positive mindset. This is called "facial feedback" and it can be a great thing to practice to lift you out of a negative way of thinking.

Our facial muscles are very responsive to our emotional state so just by changing our facial expression, we can alter our emotions. Fake smiling is effective and will also relax your facial muscles. Experiment - try to hold this smile for 5 minutes if you can. You will feel the benefit.

Surrender, acceptance and letting go

Resistance is one of the main causes of emotion. The moment we believe something isn't the way it should be, or someone doesn't meet our expectations we struggle to accept the situation because it is out of our control. We get stressed when we cannot control a person or a situation. We get frustrated because we "judge" the situation as "bad, unwanted or wrong". To combat this, we need to learn not to "feed" negative thoughts. We can do this by accepting rather than fighting a thought or emotion - accept it and then move forward. Being more aware of your thoughts on a conscious level will give you more control of your emotions by consciously changing them and not letting them spiral out of control.

Learn to accept

Learning to accept the reality of any situation or emotion and consciously choosing to view them in a different way will enable you to let go of the negative emotion you are holding on to. Learn to accept "what is" and accept that something has been and gone. Accept the emotion it may have caused you while at the same time understanding that the emotion you feel is based on a past experience, not your present reality. It does take practice but it can be very well worth it.

Meditation will help

Meditation does not stop you from thinking; we have already said that is impossible. Instead it's a practice that will help redirect your mind back to the meditation and control your thoughts and block out external influences in that time. Learn to accept your thoughts, don't judge yourself, and then refocus on a meditation or a positive thought. Mastering this will reap rewards and will begin to change your life from one of anxiety and fearfulness to one where you can concentrate on your happiness and make a peaceful and controlled place for your mind to be.

CHAPTER FIVE

*Acceptance doesn't mean resignation; it means
understanding that something is what it is and
that there's got to be a way through it.*
—Michael J. Fox

Did you know that even physical pain can be reduced by accepting it rather than resisting it? Try meditation by closing your eyes, taking a deep breath and as you slowly breath out imagine you are releasing the pain. Repeat this a few times until you come out of a resistance state of mind.

Learning how to understand and control your thoughts and emotions is also known as emotional intelligence or "EQ". Statistics show that people with a high EQ will become more successful than those with a high IQ, (intelligence quota based on academic intelligence/knowledge). Emotional intelligence can be developed and improved dramatically at any time in your life.

Think of EQ like a muscle - the more you train it, the stronger it becomes.

There is no right or wrong when it comes to emotions, they are simply reactions to what you are thinking about whether you are purposefully thinking about the cause of that emotion or not. Your belief system and unconscious thoughts happen on autopilot all the time and that is what can trigger your emotions. Sometimes, the environment we are in or people we are around can trigger emotions. This is what we call an automatic emotional response.

The importance of our "input"

Our input is made up of the things we watch on TV, read on social media, the music we listen to and the people we socialise with regularly. When we are around people on a regular basis we can be strongly influenced by their opinions, desires, actions, habits and beliefs.

We have a tendency to subconsciously believe that what the influential people in our lives desire us to do or what they perceive to be best for us is what we should do. This puts limitations on our life and can cause us to make regrettable decisions for ourselves. What defines beauty to us will be influenced by the culture we live in.

Susie is a good example. Starting at a new job she suddenly found herself in the midst of a trendy and pretty catty bunch of new colleagues. Suddenly the style she had developed for herself and that she thought suited her well did not seem to cut it. For a while she put up with the comments:

"Wow you are brave wearing that!"

"Oh goodness me I thought that style went out in the 80's?"

Susie decided that things needed to change and went about revamping her wardrobe, her vocabulary and a lot of other things about herself, to fit in. The problem was that in the process of re-inventing herself, Susie lost her identity. She got depressed and felt completely out of touch with her life. Then she met Angie. Angie had started at the same time as she had but Angie had ignored the pressures and turned up in the same outfits every day. Angie had got her fair share of comments, just as Susie had but she seemed to be accepted, and she was clearly not changing for anyone. One lunchtime Susie asked Angie how she did it and Angie told her that she practiced mindfulness. Soon Susie was practicing mindfulness and feeling the benefit. This is the way that she tackled the situation and how you can too.

First of all, take some time and actually write down on paper the story of your own personal identity. Have a go at writing down the things you are good at, things like:

- I am a good listener.
- I am a good friend.
- I have my own sense of style.
- I am a hard worker.

Then write down the things that you think have made you who you are, things from your background like:

- My mother was very kind and had time for everyone.
- My father was a very dedicated worker.
- My family were always a bit quirky.
- We moved a lot when I was young.

Once you have got down to the basics then you can really unpick who you are and what you story really is, free of the influences from those around you and from society as a whole. Then when you have all you need ask yourself the following questions:

1. How has my story evolved?
2. Is this really my story or is it a story that really someone else's?

3. Does this story truly reflect me as I am now?
4. Does this story help me to be happy or does it impede my happiness?
5. Is this the way I want to be, is it what I have dreamt of or not?
6. Should I carry on living my story or is now the time to start to write a new story?

The easiest way to work on your own personal story when you come to the conclusion that things are not going as well as you would like them to is to take a step back. Then have an objective look at your emotions and your thoughts and decide whether you have developed an attachment to a thought or emotion that really is not relevant to you, your life and your personal story anymore. If you identify that it is not, then it is time that you got the thought or emotion out of your life. Does that sound easier said than done? Well this is how you do it.

Following the steps that I outlined in the last chapter, you need to let those thoughts and emotions make an appearance, acknowledge them and then dismiss them. They do not need to be there in your consciousness but when they are in your mind is the time that you can give them their marching orders. They are no longer relevant, and they do not define you. You can let them go. Everyday thousands of thoughts and emotions go through your head and it is up to you to weed out those that are not helping you or are holding you back.

Social media – for better or worse

There is no doubt that social media has a positive side and can be beneficial and indeed it has been a lifeline to many during the Coronavirus crisis. There are many excellent uses for social media such as advertising, work, staying in contact with friends and family and uploading our favourite holiday pictures. But as we all know only too well, there is also a very negative side to social media, an impact that can have a detrimental effect on our mindset if used in the wrong way or if we become too reliant on social media platforms.

We do not have to be slaves to social media and all of us need to be mindful of what we allow to influence us and the input that we allow. Make conscious decisions about what you watch and read and whether or not you're going to let it affect you and influence your true desires and opinions.

> **Tip:** *Avoid scrolling through social media first thing in the morning and last thing at night before you go to sleep. It is far better to start your day focused and positive without seeing anything negative or upsetting. It is far better to f end your day feeling calm, positive and not influenced by other people's ideas, thoughts, dramas or gossip. Allowing these negative and worrying thoughts into your brain can ruin your day and disturb your sleep. When we sleep it is important for our unconscious mind to be focused on ourselves, our life and vision and on our own dreams. We need to be clear of the dramas and hostile utterings of other people.*

- If you are not happy with your life, you have the ability to change it. Be active, keeping your body fit and well keeps your mind in equilibrium.

- Talk about your life plans to others and let them remind you of what your goals are.

- Write a daily to do list and stick to it. This will give you a sense of achievement no matter how small the tasks.

- Have gratitude for the things and the people you appreciate in your life and realise how lucky you are to have them.

- Be present with people - don't be on your phone at the dinner table or while your spending time with your loved ones or family. If you are having a conversation be present. There is nothing worse than feeling that you have half of someone's attention because they are waiting for a tweet to be answered or a text responded to.

Interaction

- Less social media and phones will let you hear the real voices of people you care about. Listen to what they say.

- Meditate daily and take the time to sooth your body mind and soul.

Using mindfulness on a daily basis will eventually develop into a habit. Consistency is powerful. Practice mindfulness every day by using the list I have written for you above. Every morning is a new opportunity to reset and to set your mood for the day. Some of the most successful people in the world have a morning mindfulness routine, including Oprah Winfrey. Oprah Winfrey has long been on a mission with her talk shows to spread the message of health and wellness, as well as mind-body balance to everyone. Oprah has practiced meditation and mindfulness and, with spiritual gurus Deepak Chopra and Eckhart Tolle, has hosted meditation podcasts, sponsored retreats, and discussions, and credited mindfulness and meditation with changing her life and making it better. Oprah[1] explained that "meditation is about getting still enough to know the difference between the voice and you. It's a heightened state of being that lets whatever you're doing be your best life, from moment to astonishing moment."

This can be achieved in as little as 10 minutes. Plan your routine the evening before, and don't be too rigid, change it weekly or daily, tailor it to your ideal routine. Allowing some flexibility makes the process more accessible and enjoyable overall.

Gratitude

We all know what gratitude is, or at least we should do. It is having a deep appreciation, acknowledgement and thankfulness for someone or something no matter how big or small. It is a positive emotion and must be practiced daily as part of your new mindfulness routine. At the moment the gratitude that we feel to those frontline workers who have

---

[1]   Oprah and Deepak Chopra

fought the Coronavirus outbreak and continue to do so is something that we all feel and appreciate as they risk their own lives for ours. Now as the pandemic starts to recede, we must do all we can to keep fresh in our minds the gratitude we feel at this point in our history and never take for granted the sacrifices that others have made for us.

A great habit to get into is to practice writing in your journal, every day, 3 - 5 things that you are grateful for and as you write them say them in your head or say them out loud.

It could be anything and maybe at this time might look something like this:

- I am grateful for those keeping me safe from Coronavirus.
- I am grateful that I am well.
- I am grateful that my family are well.
- I am grateful that I have a garden where I can relax.
- I am grateful for friends.

It doesn't always have to be the big-ticket items, small things like enjoying a coffee or a chat with a friend you have not spoken to for a while can count too!

Psychology research shows that feeling gratitude helps people have more positive emotions, enhance good experiences, improve health and build stronger relationships.

Meditation

Let's be clear for all those who haven't used meditation before: meditation is not a form of religion, nor is it only practiced by religious or spiritual people and it's not only practiced at the top of a mountain cross-legged, at sunrise! It is true that meditation is practiced more regularly by people of certain cultures and religions, but anyone can use meditation no matter what their beliefs are. Meditation is a practice where you focus on a particular thought, object, activity or sound to refocus and to quieten the mind and train it into attention and awareness. This will lead to the achievement of a mentally clear and emotionally calm state of mind.

Looking inward

Meditation is a formal practice that should be directed internally to reduce your level of thinking and NOT to force yourself to completely stop thinking. People have a preconception of meditation and typically if this is portrayed in the media it will be against a serene backdrop with the meditator sitting in certain poses, palms up and a serene expression on their face. In fact, you don't need to be in any particular position to meditate and you don't need to be flexible. It is about just being still and comfortable, so that you have no distractions. You can meditate sitting up or lying down. Meditation is also often used by people suffering chronic pain to reduce discomfort.

Practicing your own meditation can be just as powerful and healing as a guided meditation once it becomes part of your life. I change my meditations daily to fit what is in my mind or what I want to manifest for myself. For example, if I want more energy in the morning, I will put on some background meditation music and close my eyes, then take 3 deep breathes and imagine a blue energy coming into the crown of my head and circulating to every part of my body.

Or if I want to manifest more happiness for myself, I will imagine a golden light throughout my body and repeat some affirmations in my head, such as:

HAPPINESS IS A MAGNET TO ME

HAPPINESS FLOWS TO ME COPIOUSLY AND ENDLESSLY

It takes more concentration but it's worth it as I feel so lifted, energised and motivated afterwards.

Establishing a formal meditation practice

Before you start your own meditation regime, ask yourself these questions:

- What is the reason you want to establish a meditation practice? Is it to manage pain? Reduce stress? To relax? To manifest or get yourself into a positive vibration? There are so many reasons people meditate and so many things it can help with.
- What benefits do you hope to receive from your

meditation practice?

- How much time per day can you commit to your meditation? Once a day for 5 minutes or twice a day for 10 minutes?
- How will you be able to develop your meditation into a daily habit/routine?

Tips to help you succeed

- You could attach your meditation to another existing pattern, such as after brushing your teeth each morning and when you get into bed in the evening.
- Schedule your meditation – set a phone reminder or put it on your to do list daily, or in your planner.
- Are you going to sit somewhere comfortably or lie down? Identify a specific place where you can meditate where you will be undisturbed.

I found it an important part of healing and practicing this new way of life to have a routine, and practice being mindful on a daily basis. I started by meditating once a day and writing down five things I am grateful for each morning and I practiced being mindful in my passing thoughts. I wrote in my diary and set reminders and I stuck to it. Consistency is key.

CHAPTER SIX

*If every eight-year-old in the world is taught
meditation, we will eliminate violence from
the world within one generation.*

— Dali Lama

Where do we start?

Where do we start with meditation? These are my suggestions for you if you want to start your own meditation routine.

- Decide what your main focus is for your meditation.
- Decide how long you want it to be.
- Research phone apps and videos online such as YouTube for guided meditations and various practices.
- Don't **ever** drive or operate machinery while meditating.
- Always check how long a guided meditation is and check that you have time to do it, you don't want to have to stop halfway.
- Think about an energy meditation, a positive thinking or healing meditation.
- If you want to practice meditation to help with anxiety or stress, look out for those.
- You could do meditations with affirmations or to attract abundance or love.

You will find your favourites, and what works best for you. I have favourites where I find particular voices or sounds more relaxing; one of my personal favourites is Bob Proctor. You can find his meditations on YouTube.

Think about your own beliefs and the goals that you have and then customise your mindfulness experience to what you need. For example, if you are more spiritual or if you feel that you want to be more in touch with the universe you can use more spiritual meditations. If you feel that you are sometimes overwhelmed by emotions of a past or present event, then you might find it too painful to be very introspective. Once you have identified what is at the root of your unhappiness you should then be able to direct your attention to the present time and, using the techniques I have taught you, try to bring your attention back to the present moment and move forward from there.

Digging deeper

For some of you, however, it may actually help to look deeper into your feelings and maybe change how you perceive something. For example, if a certain situation made us feel angry or upset or anxious, as we touched on earlier, if we allow those feelings to come and go then we are bringing our awareness to our emotions and the physical sensations of them, and this will bring us into the present moment. Now we are prevented from getting carried away by the feelings as we are in control and we can let those feelings go rather than letting them run away with us.

If you find yourself extremely overwhelmed with fear and panic, it is best to come away from the emotion and divert the thought process to the story and not the feeling. If you choose to meditate when you're feeling this way, your attention will be diverted, and you will calm down so you can think more clearly.

Let's look at an example by Ali Woo[1]:

"If you've ever suffered with chronic anxiety, you know the horrible effect that it can have on your life. The stress, heartache and mental anguish of constant fear is something you're probably familiar with. It can be devastating, affecting your career and relationships. In my own life, anxiety contributed to a number of issues; having trouble with developing close personal relationships, fear of overcrowded areas (yes, anxiety intensified my agoraphobia), overeating, over-stimulation which made focusing difficult at best and contributed to an increase in panic attacks and asthma. Couple all of that with university, owning and managing businesses, a full-time job, marriage problems, family drama, bills and piling debt, terrible in-laws and more - I was no longer a healthy person, mentally or physically."

Woo tells us that she came to the realisation that what needed to change to relieve her suffering was the internal, not the external. She had been on medication from the doctor for her anxiety for some time but found that they made her feel dull and wooly headed and that the underlying anxiety was still there. Woo tells us that she took steps to help herself once she took the decision to stop the medication. They were:

- Cutting down on caffeine.
- Drinking herbal teas with chamomile, lavender and peppermint.
- She began to take more regular exercise, doing a lot of walking and hiking.

---

1   *How Meditation Helped Me Defeat 16 Years of Anxiety - Ali Woo*

- Woo went out and communed with nature and found her stress reduced.
- She rescued a dog.
- She did exercises that involved slow breathing.
- She even went to see a therapist.

These were all good steps for Woo, but it was not until sometime later when she went to a bookstore and happened to see a book on a table that things really changed. The cover had a picture of a Buddhist monk in wonderfully colourful robes. He was laughing and his eyes were closed as he sat, his legs crossed. Woo tells us that the book was entitled Joyful Wisdom, by Yongey Mingyur Rinpoche & Eric Swanson, and it introduced her to the art of meditation. It is at this point in her article that Woo warns that with the many different types of meditation it is important to know that although some are wonderful, others can lead you down the wrong path. Woo quotes Lucans Chu who is a practitioner and teacher and says simply:

"Meditation can bring on negative associations to some people. This is the fault of borderline cult organizations, quasi-religious groups, "new age" jargon, paid celebrity endorsements, false "gurus", impossible guarantees and poorly taught practices. However, when practiced correctly, meditation is one of the most powerful exercises. It is a practice that has been utilized across the world for millennia."

There is no need to jump into a meditation centre and Woo tells us that she started her meditation in her own bedroom.

"Meditation is very intimate, because it is one of the few, if

only times, we sit down and have a "conversation" of sorts with our minds. Getting to know the inner workings of our minds is the first step in meditation and requires being completely open and accepting of the things your mind shows you, whether it is good or bad. With enough practice, you will learn not only to pinpoint your anxiety issues, but to face them and accept them as you would a friend."

When you start to meditate you will realise just how busy your brain is, communicating with you constantly and processing the events of your day so that you can make sense of it.

Woo tells us that if she has not meditated for a while, she finds her mind is confused and busy with her thoughts and she needs to train herself again to have the open and quiet mind that will allow her to have a healing process through meditation.

There is no doubt that it does take time, when you first start meditation or if you stop for a while, to get yourself into the right receptive place for that meditation again. But the benefits will be well worth the effort. Your health will improve, and you will feel more in control of your emotions. People will notice the new you and how relaxed and together you are. Woo also points out that one of the big advantages of meditation is getting to know your own mind really well.

How will mindfulness and meditation bring change into my life?

When you practice meditation and mindfulness you will begin to deal with stress, changes and challenges on an emotional and physical level differently than you have before. Not only that, you will look at the bigger picture, be at peace and accept things better by being able to look at different perspectives and by not letting your thoughts and emotions run away with you. You will be more present with people and more focused and aware of situations knowing that you can change them and alter your outlook on things to let go and move forward. You will feel empowered, calm and in control.

Being active is an important part of mindfulness and healing

The word 'motion' is part of the word "emotion" and that is because it can be moved. Moving physically can change the emotional pattern in your mind and body. Each emotion we have has a physical response, for example when we are scared our heart beats faster or we begin to sweat. When we are anxious or nervous, we may get an uneasy feeling in our tummy or be restless and unable to stay still.

This brings us back to the benefit of the 'fake smile' which is a perfect example of how moving in certain ways can change our emotions and how we feel. When we smile, our brain releases feel-good chemicals because of our mouth movement. Going for walks and doing daily exercise can help with stress and anxiety and it benefits your mental and physical health in a huge way.

Becoming spiritual

Let's talk about being or becoming spiritual, especially for those who are new to the concept of spirituality. Being spiritual does not mean you have to be religious or follow any particular belief system. The word 'spiritual' has been used as a way of describing the many and various aspects that go to make up 'religion' for many years. Spirituality is now becoming associated with the interior life of a person and it places an emphasis on the wellbeing of the mind, body and spirit. When people describe a "spiritual awakening" it usually means that they have a newfound awareness of spiritual reality.

The awakened state embraces all experiences and states of awareness. With it you will feel a new sense of energy and purpose and lose the constant need for something to fulfil you. We have already said that overeating, drinking, drug taking, and many other destructive things are a consequence of searching to fill a void.

People who practice mindfulness and meditation will often describe how they begin to feel more spiritually connected as they become more focused and energised and less concerned about society and other people's beliefs and opinions. It is a very good place to be.

The Law of Attraction

So now that you have learned about understanding and controlling your emotions and you know how to practice putting yourself into a positive mind-set and raising your vibration, you have started to practice mindfulness and meditation and you may well be intrigued about the idea of becoming more spiritual if you aren't already. You might very possibly want to know more about the secret to a happier and fulfilled life. The Law of Attraction is a vital element of this. Mindfulness and meditation are key factors to incorporating the Law of Attraction into your life.

What is it?

What exactly is the Law of Attraction? The Law of Attraction is the ability to attract positivity to our lives by focusing on our wants and making these a reality. This happens naturally and you will establish your own Law of Attraction every single day. Sounds good? Well it should be but the problem is that many people unintentionally focus on what they do not want rather than what they do want. The solution is to send out a higher frequency of positivity to squash the negativity, so this does not fester in your thoughts. If you are constantly thinking, "what if it all goes wrong?" you will start visualising all of the ways that the relationship, the job or the trip will not work. The universe will not hear the "what if" part of your thought, it will simply bring you the negative things that you are thinking of. Whatever you visualize on and whatever your focus on, is exactly what you will attract and bring into your life. Given that we do tend to dwell on the negative it can be tough to try and ignore those negative trains of thought. If you can do it, it will be well worth it.

Plug into that positive frequency because you have the ability to give out a much more powerful signal and attract positivity far better than you would attract the negative.

What is the secret?

The secret is this: if a negative thought does pass through your mind, you have time to change what is manifested from that negative thought by changing it to a positive one and making the "feeling" or the "frequency" of that thought so strong that it will drown out the negative.

No one actively seeks negative thinking, so it can often be considered unintentional. That means that those thoughts are not as powerful because we are simply listening to them and accepting their presence and not purposely putting intention or energy into them. By using positive thinking, we can intentionally put thought and passion into converting those negative thoughts into positively embracing constructive thoughts because this high energy happy vibration is **much** more powerful.

The Law of Attraction will not work instantly so I always say to people that they should not be alarmed if they are reliving any kind of bad scenario, no matter how deeply entrenched it seems to be, because it is never too late to put all your focus into the best-case scenario. How? By using meditations, affirmations and really changing that negative thought into a powerful, positive high vibrational one, will make the Law of Attraction work for you and bring you the positive things in your life that you most desire.

OUR MIND WORKS IN PICTURES, SO WHAT YOU PICTURE, BECOMES A REALITY.

Always remember that **"a thought is NOT a truth."** Don't get muddled up with your thought process and how the Law of Attraction works. For example, "I feel depressed today." This is not a truth; this is a thought and an opinion and an outlook on a thought you have. Thoughts only become real if you allow or choose them to be. Sound radical? I am sure it does because we are not taught that our thoughts do not have to be considered true or that we can control our minds. Your thought process is the biggest part of the Law of Attraction. You need a high energy and vibration to process your thoughts appropriately.

To gain the good things that you want in your life, you need your thoughts to be passionate, stimulating, energetic and positive. You need to really think about it in depth and feel it. Manifesting is when our desires become visible. Thought is a key element in a humans ability to create. We generate a thought and the universe receives it, and so our lives are a reflection of our thoughts.

If I asked you what the strongest parts of your body are you might say your arms and legs or maybe your back. Well you would be wrong. The two most powerful parts of our body are our hearts and our minds.

CHAPTER SEVEN

The state of your life is nothing more than
a reflection of your state of mind.
— Wayne W Dyer

Our hearts give off emotional energy through electrical pulses, and they react with our emotions. Our brains also work through electrical pulses and through energy generated by our thoughts. If you can manage to align the two then you will see how your life can change. Your heart and mind combining their energy is a formidable force and gives off the most powerful energy. And don't just take my word for it, it has been scientifically proven.

A Gaia article published online in January 2020 described that the human heart, that is actually the size of two fists, has many features such as intelligence, mystery and power and often the completely inexplicable.

The ancient Egyptians believed that the God of the underworld Anubis, who was also judge of the dead, would weigh the hearts of anyone who died against the weight of a feather and if the two were found to be in balance the owner could have their heart back. If the heart was found to be heavier than a feather, then it was thought this was due to being weighed down by bad deeds that had been committed throughout the person's life. In this case the heart would be fed to a monster.

Does the heart rule the brain?

Ancient philosopher Aristotle attributed reason, emotion and thought to our hearts rather than our brains. In the ninth century Abu Nasr al-Farabi, an Arabic philosopher said that he believed, "the ruling organ in the human body is the heart; the brain is a secondary ruling organ subordinated to the heart." Later, in the 19th century Auguste Comte, who was a French philosopher, believed that the brain was the heart's servant. There have been many other ideas put forward as to the function and the connection between our hearts and our minds.

The brain-heart connection

As you are reading this your heart is beating at a rate that is double that of most other animals. Also interesting is the fact that humans are prone to vascular disease while this was not found in our closest ancestors, the great apes.

As it has its own electrical impulse, the heart of a human being will continue to beat even when it's taken out of the human body. Additionally, if human hearts are grown in the laboratory, the cells will synchronise with each other in their motion. The electrical frequency emitted by the heart has a frequency that is thousands of times more powerful anything else in our body.

Brain power

Meanwhile in our brain, neurons take on the responsibility of processing and sending messages to our bodies such as, 'reach out your hand and open the door'. Neurons are also responsible for transmitting our emotions and the specialised cells that are needed for this are found in the nervous system, the brain but also in the heart. These cells cause the coherence between the brain and the heart. From this you will see there can be no dispute that the heart and the brain are connected in more ways than just the physiological.

Happiness and heartache

There was a recent study showing that the emotion of extreme anger or of grief can do severe damage to the heart and there is evidence to suggest that people are more likely to have a heart attack in the aftermath of a loved one dying. At the other extreme, joy and happiness show evidence of coherent rhythms within the heart. We know that the endocrine system is responsible for producing hormones, but I wonder how many of us knew that oxytocin which is also known as the 'love hormone' is actually made within the heart.

In pursuit of the resonance of hearts and minds

There have been many studies done that document the profound benefits that meditation can have. There are the physical benefits of reduced anxiety, relief from depression, lower blood pressure, increased brain matter and pain relief. When people meditate, they achieve heart and brain coherence where the heart will be moved into a different state and that coherence is a synchronised brain and heart neurology. This will not be the same through every type of meditation, for instance, a mindfulness meditation will produce a different signature than a loving kindness meditation.

Here is one way in which to trigger that heart/brain synchronisation:

- Choose the peaceful quiet place.
- Clear your mind of all external influences.
- Focus on your heart, feel it beating.
- Concentrate on feeling compassion.
- Think about that feeling flooding through you and radiating out to other people.

Carrying out this simple meditation can not only relieve anxiety and depression and stress but will also achieve heart and brain coherence.

There are four words that can trigger your coherence and they are compassion, gratitude, care and appreciation. If you focus your meditation along the feeling of one of these words or combinations of them, you will open the lines of communication between your heart and your brain. It will take about three days to create a neuron pathway or habitual pattern that will support your new heart to brain communication and connection. Here are some things to bear in mind:

- The universe does not recognise time.
- Be ready but do not expect results straight away.
- The universe does not recognise size.
- The universe works through vibration and energy.
- You need to be specific when you meditate and know

what you truly desire.

- You need to be consistent, and committed.
- You need to form a new habit of thinking and take action every day to manifest using mindfulness and meditation practices.
- You must put in the time, energy and effort to reap the reward.

So, after all that, here is the fun part... What exactly do you want? After all, you are the creator of your own life.

When you are manifesting you must always state what you want in the present tense and with gratitude. For example, *"I am so grateful for the financial abundance the universe has brought to me."*

While you meditate and invite the manifestation of your dreams and desires, it is not enough to just to speak the words, you must feel it, believe it and put it into a context as though what you wanted was already here. Remember, your brain does not know the difference between reality and imagination. If you approach your meditation and manifestation in this way you will give off the right energy and frequency by doing this and that will attract the things you want to you.

Feel it!

So how will you feel when you receive what you have wished for? Try this:

- Close your eyes and imagine how it will feel to receive

your dream and the things in your life that you are seeking to manifest.

- Write down what you want, including emotionally, materialistically and maybe even experiences you wish you could have.
- Write down what you want in detail, even making a vision board. Do you want to own your own home? Visualise it, how it is decorated, where it is, what the garden looks like and write it down in every detail.

Vision boarding is very important when you are manifesting. You can do this by making a vision album on your phone, your computer or on paper. Once you have made it up then it should:

- Reflect what you want in your life.
- Use words and emotions that you want to feel and bring into your life.
- Be somewhere where you will see it every day.
- Be available for you to look at several times a day to remind yourself what you are working towards.

Pay attention to any opportunities that arise. Take action now. Do not put it off until tomorrow or the next day. Opportunities will begin to arise as soon as you have raised your vibration and you need to be ready to take advantage of them.

You must be mindful of your thoughts and not let fear get in the way. Those thoughts might be things like:

"I can't do that."

"I'm not good enough."

"I don't deserve it."

"It won't work."

These are destructive thoughts that you can change. Use affirmations. Say to yourself in your head or out loud.

"I *am* good enough."

"This *can* work."

"*Everyone* deserves happiness."

"I *am* doing this!"

Be excited and focused. It is very true that our mind can play tricks on us and make us full of doubt. It is important to remember that none of these doubts are real, most of them come from others, their opinions and the importance that we wrongly attach to that. This is about you not them and you can banish those thoughts of self-doubt and leave them behind with the people who would seek to derail you either directly or indirectly with their expectations and beliefs.

Do not let other people's negativity get in your way. If you receive negative feedback about an idea, thought or a belief, come away from the conversation keeping your own ideas and thoughts strong and positive. Remember that you can always silence negative thoughts with new affirmations.

Affirmations are also important in that you can repeat your desires once or even a few times daily. Doing this will put these ideas into your unconscious mind, not just your consciousness. Some affirmations that I use regularly are:

"I live in optimum health."

"I attract wealth."

"I am a magnet to happiness."

"I am successful and driven."

"I attract love."

The strength of your thought/beliefs is important, the more you feel what you are thinking, the more the universe will respond to you. By using affirmations and repeating positive thoughts you make those thoughts and your desires stronger and stronger until they become a reality in your life.

Gratitude

Gratitude is a very important part of manifesting. As soon as you begin to change your expectations to appreciation the universe will bring more goodness into your life and that is why you must practice gratitude daily. This practice will also help with anxiety and depression and it can shut doors on negative thoughts.

Believe

Underlying your meditation, your mindfulness and your manifestation should always be your faith and belief in the universe as well as your irrevocable belief in the Law of Attraction. After all, there is science to back up the reality of "beyond the thought". People have tested and proven the

Law of Attraction works over many years. It takes practice, persistence and it takes commitment to change your way of thinking. As Henry Ford once said, "thinking is the hardest work there is, which is probably the reason that only a few are dedicated to it!"

Meditate and be mindful

I cannot put enough emphasis on the excellent benefits you will get from using mindfulness and meditation. People are sometimes intimidated by it just because they don't know how it works, but now you have the tools and knowledge and know how to put these invaluable practices into effect. Done properly and with commitment, it will reset you, energise you, bring out your strongest inner self and bring you creativity beyond what you have ever even imagined yourself capable of.

These are a few points that we have already touched on, but I would like to mention again.

- You do not have to follow any religion to be spiritual; being spiritual is not a religion.
- A religion is an organised system of beliefs, ceremonies & rules used to worship a god or multiple gods that incorporates spirituality but that does not have exclusivity over it.
- Spirituality seen in basic terms is relating to, consisting of or affecting the spirit.
- Spirituality is feeling connected with the universe and

being connected with a power greater than ourselves.

I believe in Teilhard de Chardins statement:

"WE ARE NOT HUMAN BEINGS HAVING A SPIRITUAL EXPERIENCE, WE ARE SPIRITUAL BEINGS HAVING A HUMAN EXPERIENCE."

These are some thoughts that we should all have in our minds, especially when we consider the way that the world has been affected by the Coronavirus pandemic.

- Regardless of how challenging your destiny might be, you should never give up.
- The world needs you now more than ever to mentor, guide, heal and help one another Set examples.
- Be yourself and do not contribute to negativity.
- Making a decision is the only way we can make a change in our lives.
- Be committed, set goals, have targets and when you reach them set them again and aim higher. Challenge yourself!
- You have to be able to see what doesn't exist. What other people may perceive as impossible; you will see as possible. Your mind is your creator.
- Everybody has time. You make time.
- There's nothing you cannot do and nothing you cannot be.
- Make a conscious choice to change and succeed. You're the only one who can make this choice; no one is going

to do it for you.
- Don't keep reliving experiences over and over again unless they make you smile, laugh or feel joy and fulfilment.

FURTHER READING

1. *The Secret* – Rhonda Byrne
2. Oprah.com – Oprah Winfrey & Deepak Chopra
3. *How Mediation Helped me Defeat 16 Years of Anxiety* – Ali Woo
4. *Joyful Wisdom* – Yongey Mingyur Rinpache & Eric Swanson
5. Science of Mind Youtube Channel – Joe Dispenza

If you would like further help with mindfulness or life coaching, please contact me through my business pages.

Email jem.lifecoach@gmail.com
Instagram @jema_lifecoach
Facebook @jem.lifecoach